The Gospel of Mary Magdalene

Mystical Teachings on Love, Wisdom, and Inner Transformation

A Modern Translation

Adapted for the Contemporary Reader

Mary Magdalene

Translated by Tim Zengerink

© **Copyright 2025**
All rights reserved.

It is not legal to reproduce, duplicate, or transmit any part of this document in either electronic means or in printed format. Recording of this publication is strictly prohibited and any storage of this document is not allowed unless with written permission from the publisher except for the use of brief quotations in a book review.

This book contains works of fiction. Any resemblance to persons living or dead, or places, events, or locations is purely coincidental.

Table Of Contents

Preface - Message to the Reader 1

Introduction 5

Chapter 4 12

Chapter 5 15

Chapter 8 18

Chapter 9 21

Thank You for Reading 23

Preface - Message to the Reader

What If You Could Help Rebuild the Greatest Library in Human History?

Thousands of years ago, the Library of Alexandria stood as the crown jewel of human achievement — a sanctuary where the collected wisdom of every known civilization was gathered, preserved, and shared freely.

And then, it was lost.

Through fire, conquest, and the slow erosion of time, humanity lost not just books — but ideas, dreams, discoveries, and stories that could have changed the world forever.

Today, the Library of Alexandria lives again — and you are invited to be a part of its restoration.

Our mission is simple yet profound:

To rebuild the greatest library the world has ever known, and to translate all timeless works into every language and dialect, so that no seeker of knowledge is ever left behind again.

By joining our movement to rebuild the modern Library of Alexandria, you become part of an unprecedented mission:

- **Unlimited Access to the Greatest Audiobooks & eBooks Ever Written:**

  Instantly explore thousands of legendary works—Plato, Shakespeare, Jane Austen, Leo Tolstoy, and countless more. All instantly available to read or listen, placing a complete literary universe at your fingertips.

- **Beautiful Paperback & Deluxe Editions at Printing Cost**

  Own any title as an elegant paperback, deluxe hardcover, or stunning collectible boxset—offered to you at true printing cost, delivered straight to your door. Build your personal Library of Alexandria, crafted for beauty, built for durability, and worthy of proud display.

- **Fresh Translations for Modern Readers—in Every Language & Dialect**

  Enjoy timeless masterpieces reimagined in clear, contemporary language—no more outdated phrases or obscure references. Alongside the original versions, we're tirelessly translating these classics into every language and dialect imaginable, ensuring accessibility and understanding across cultures and generations.

- **Join a Global Renaissance of Literature & Knowledge**

    You directly support expanding our library, publishing deluxe editions at true cost, translating works into all global languages, and bringing humanity's greatest stories to people everywhere. By joining today, you're not just preserving a legacy of masterpieces; you set in motion a powerful wave of literary accessibility.

Become a Torchbearer of Knowledge.

Join us for free now at LibraryofAlexandria.com

Together, we will ensure that the light of human wisdom never fades again.

With gratitude and a shared love of knowledge,

The Modern Library of Alexandria Team

Visit:

www.libraryofalexandria.com

Or scan the code below:

Introduction

The Voice of the Soul and the Path to Inner Knowing

The Gospel of Mary Magdalene is one of the most luminous and empowering texts to have emerged from the early Christian mystical tradition. Though fragmented and long hidden from public view, this gospel reveals the voice of a woman who was not only a close follower of Jesus but also a profound spiritual teacher in her own right. It offers us a rare glimpse into a vision of Christianity that centers on inner awakening, self-knowledge, and divine union—one that is contemplative, inclusive, and radically transformative.

Attributed to Mary Magdalene, this gospel stands apart from the canonical texts not because it contradicts their essential message of love and grace, but because it reveals a deeper, more inward dimension of spiritual transformation. Rather than focusing on external laws or historical events, The Gospel of Mary Magdalene turns our gaze inward—to the soul's journey through suffering, ignorance, and fear, and toward a state of inner peace and divine awareness. It invites us not to follow a path imposed from without, but to remember who we truly are—to awaken to the light and wisdom that already dwell within us.

This gospel begins in the aftermath of Jesus' resurrection, when the disciples, filled with confusion and fear, ask Mary to share the teachings the Savior revealed to her in private. What follows is a dialogue on the nature of the soul, the illusion of sin, the path of ascent through the spiritual realms, and the healing power of knowledge and love. Mary does not present herself as a rival to Peter or the other apostles, but as a bearer of inner truth—a truth born of direct experience, personal transformation, and deep spiritual communion with the divine.

One of the central teachings in this text is that salvation is not achieved through suffering or external sacrifice, but through gnosis—inner knowing. The soul, according to Mary, must confront and overcome the powers that seek to bind it in fear, desire, and ignorance. These are not merely cosmic forces, but aspects of our own inner life—emotional and psychological barriers that keep us from realizing our divine origin. As the soul moves beyond these barriers, it comes into full awareness of its unity with the Source. This is not a doctrine of separation, but of return. Not punishment, but liberation. Not fear, but love.

The gospel's voice is quiet, yet revolutionary. It elevates the feminine, not in opposition to the masculine, but as an essential and equal partner in the divine order. It honors inner wisdom over external authority. It affirms that the soul's journey is not to be dictated by dogma, but discovered through relationship—with the self, with others, and with the divine presence that lives in all beings. It presents Mary Magdalene not only as a disciple, but as a spiritual exemplar—one who understands that the true temple is within, and that enlightenment begins with listening deeply to the voice of the soul.

Reclaiming Mary Magdalene's Wisdom and Presence

For centuries, Mary Magdalene's role in Christian history was obscured, distorted, and diminished. Often misidentified as a repentant prostitute or merely a background figure, her presence was reduced to a symbol of sin and redemption, rather than honored as a bearer of sacred knowledge. Yet the discovery of The Gospel of Mary Magdalene, along with other Gnostic and early Christian texts, has reawakened interest in her authentic voice and spiritual legacy. What we find in this gospel is a woman of strength, compassion, and vision—someone who grasped the essence of Jesus' teachings and lived them with deep integrity.

In many ways, this gospel challenges the traditional structures of authority that have long defined Christian orthodoxy. It reveals a community in tension—where Peter and others question Mary's authority, even as she speaks with clarity and grace. But the gospel does not present this tension as cause for division. Instead, it portrays the path of spiritual leadership as one rooted in inner experience and divine intimacy. Mary speaks not to win argument, but to guide others toward the truth she has seen. Her presence reminds us that true spiritual authority arises not from titles or institutions, but from the authenticity of the heart.

In the teachings of Mary, we see a vision of the divine that is deeply relational. God is not a distant judge but a loving source to which the soul longs to return. The journey of the soul is not a path of shame or guilt, but of remembering—of awakening to our original wholeness. This perspective shifts the focus of the spiritual life away from fear and external control, and toward empowerment, healing, and personal transformation.

This gospel also presents an alternative view of sin—not as an offense to be punished, but as ignorance to be healed. When the soul forgets its origin, it becomes entangled in the lower passions and illusions of the material world. But through insight, contemplation, and love, it can rise again. This is the path that Mary describes—a path not of denial, but of integration. Not of condemnation, but of compassion. It is a path that honors the complexity of human experience while pointing always toward the eternal light within.

This modern translation has been prepared to bring the beauty, clarity, and wisdom of The Gospel of Mary Magdalene into accessible form for today's readers. Every sentence has been translated with attention to meaning, tone, and spiritual resonance, preserving the mystery and elegance of the original while ensuring that its teachings speak clearly and powerfully. The structure of the gospel, with its interruptions and fragmentary form, has also been honored as part of its sacred rhythm—a reflection of the soul's own journey through loss, insight, and remembrance.

To read this gospel is to enter into a sacred dialogue—not only with Mary Magdalene, but with the deeper parts of your own being. It is to hear the voice of wisdom speaking through silence, guiding you not to look outward for salvation, but inward for the light that never fades. It is to discover that the true gospel is not merely a message written in ancient words, but a living presence within you, waiting to be known.

Translated by Tim Zengerink

Let this book be your companion on the path of awakening. Let Mary's voice echo in your heart. Let her questions become your questions, and her answers your own insights. And may the journey it inspires lead you to a deeper understanding of love, wisdom, and the sacred truth of who you are.

(Pages 1 to 6 of the manuscript,
containing chapters 1 - 3, are lost.
The extant text starts on page 7...)

Chapter 4

Will the physical world eventually be destroyed, or will it last forever?

The Savior answered, "Everything in nature—every form, every creature—is connected and depends on each other. But in the end, all things will return to where they came from, back to their original source. Matter itself cannot be destroyed, but it will go back to where it began. Each part of creation is naturally drawn back to its own origin, and when it returns, it becomes whole again."

Then He said, "If you have ears, listen carefully and understand."

Peter, wanting to learn more, asked, "Since you have taught us so much, please tell us this: What is the sin of the world?"

The Savior replied, "Sin is not something that was placed on the world. It is not an outside force—it comes from human actions. Sin happens when people go against their true nature, when they act in ways that are not in harmony with how things were meant to be. This is why acts like adultery are considered sin—they are not part of the original design."

He continued, "The Good has entered the world to restore everything to its rightful place. That is the purpose of divine intervention—to bring all things back to where they belong, to heal what is broken, and to recover what was lost.

"This is also why people get sick and die. You are missing the presence of the One who has the power to heal you. When you lose that connection, you are separated from the source of life."

He added, "If you have the mind to understand, think deeply about these truths."

The Savior then explained further, "Matter itself gave rise to desires that were never meant to exist. These desires create chaos and disrupt the natural order. They bring disorder to all of creation. That is why I have told you, 'Do not be afraid.' And when you do feel discouraged, find strength in the beauty and balance of nature. Everything is part of a greater design, and in the end, all things will return to harmony."

Once more, He said, "If you have ears, truly listen and understand."

When the Blessed One finished teaching, He spoke with deep peace, saying, "Peace be with you. Take my peace into your hearts and carry it within you. Be careful of those who try to mislead you by saying, 'Look over here!' or 'Look over there!' The Son of Man is not found in such places. He is within you. Seek Him inside yourself, for those who truly look for Him will find Him."

The Savior then told them, "Go and share the good news of the Kingdom. Tell this truth to everyone who will listen. Do not create extra rules or burdens beyond what I have taught you. Do not set up laws like the old lawgivers did, or you will trap yourselves and others with unnecessary restrictions. The path I have given you is enough."

After saying this, He left them, filling them with peace and the wisdom of His words.

Chapter 5

The disciples were filled with sorrow. Their hearts felt heavy as they cried and mourned, saying, "How can we go out and share the message of the Son of Man with those who do not know Him? If they did not spare Him, our Savior, why would they treat us any differently? Surely, we will suffer just as He did."

Then Mary stood up among them, her presence strong and steady. She greeted them warmly and said, "My brothers, do not weep, and do not let grief take over your hearts. Do not lose hope or let fear stop you. The grace of the Savior will stay with you. It will protect you and guide you in the mission He has given you."

She continued, "Instead of focusing on sorrow, let us give thanks and praise for all He has done. He has prepared us for this. He has changed us, making us strong so that we can continue His work."

Her words brought them comfort, and as she spoke, their sadness began to fade. The disciples felt their hearts turning back toward the truth. They started to reflect on the Savior's teachings, feeling a new sense of purpose.

Peter then turned to Mary and said, "Sister, we

know that the Savior thought highly of you, that He loved you more than the other women. You understand His teachings more deeply than we do. Please, share with us what He told you—things that we have not heard. Teach us what has been hidden from us."

Mary, calm and confident, replied, "What you do not know, I will now reveal to you. These are the things I have kept close to my heart, and I will share them so that you too may understand."

She then began to speak. "I saw the Lord in a vision. I said to Him, 'Lord, today I saw You in a vision.' He answered me, 'Blessed are you, Mary, because you believed what you saw without doubting. Where your mind is focused, there your treasure will also be.'"

I asked Him, 'Lord, when someone sees a vision, how do they perceive it? Through the soul, or through the spirit?'

The Savior replied, 'It is not through the soul or the spirit that visions are seen. It is through the mind, which exists between the two. The mind is like a bridge, connecting what is seen to what is understood. Through it, true wisdom is revealed.'"

Mary paused, her words carrying deep meaning. The disciples sat in silence, reflecting on what she had shared, trying to grasp the mystery of her vision and the wisdom of the Savior's teaching.

(pages 11-14 are missing from the manuscript)

Chapter 8

Desire confronted the soul and said, "I didn't see you when you first entered the world, but now I see you leaving it. Why are you trying to trick me? You belong to me—you always have."

But the soul stood firm and replied, "I saw you, but you never truly saw me or understood who I am. I wrapped myself around you like a garment, covering you, but you never recognized my purpose or my presence."

After saying this, the soul moved forward, filled with joy and victory.

As it ascended, the soul encountered the third force, Ignorance. This power blocked its way and demanded, "Where do you think you're going? You are trapped in darkness and cannot escape. You are bound by sin, so you have no right to judge."

The soul replied with confidence, "Why do you accuse me when I have judged no one? I was trapped by forces I did not choose, but I have never trapped anyone. You did not recognize me, but I have come to recognize you. Now I see that everything—the heavens and the earth—is returning to its true source."

Having overcome Ignorance, the soul gained even more strength and determination. It then came upon the fourth power, a great force that appeared in seven different forms:

1. Darkness, blinding the way and creating fear.
2. Desire, overwhelming and consuming.
3. Ignorance, spreading confusion and doubt.
4. Fear of death, shaking the soul with terror.
5. The rule of the flesh, tempting with worldly pleasures.
6. False wisdom, pretending to hold knowledge but offering nothing.
7. Anger and pride, burning with destruction and arrogance.

These seven forces together made up the power of Wrath, standing in the soul's path to challenge its journey.

They spoke, accusing the soul, "Where do you come from, you who have defied us? And where do you think you are going? You dare to rise above the powers that rule this world?"

The soul stood strong and answered without fear, "The things that once held me back have no power over me anymore. I have overcome them. My desires have faded, and ignorance has been destroyed."

The soul continued, "I no longer belong to this world. I am free from the chains of illusion and forgetfulness that once kept me trapped. These things are temporary, but I am not. Now, I will rise to a place of eternal peace, a realm beyond time, where everything is whole and unchanging."

With these words, the soul broke free from the grasp of the powers, rising beyond their reach. It entered the eternal light, where it finally found true rest.

Chapter 9

When Mary finished speaking, she became silent because that was all the Savior had shared with her.

But Andrew turned to the others and said, "Say what you think about what she just said. But I don't believe the Savior actually said this. These ideas seem strange to me."

Then Peter also spoke, responding to the same discussion.

He questioned them, saying, "Could the Savior really have spoken privately with a woman and not to us? Are we supposed to listen to her now? Did He really choose her over us?"

Mary started to cry and said to Peter, "My brother Peter, do you really think I made this up? Do you believe I am lying about what the Savior said?"

Levi then spoke up and said to Peter, "Peter, you have always been quick to anger."

"Now I see you attacking this woman just like our enemies would."

"But if the Savior considered her worthy, who are you to reject her? Surely, He knows her well."

"That is why He loved her more than us. Instead of arguing, we should be ashamed of our doubts and focus on becoming the true people He called us to be. Let's go our separate ways as He commanded and preach the gospel, without adding any extra rules or laws beyond what the Savior taught."

After hearing this, they went out and began spreading His message.

Thank You for Reading

Dear Reader,

We hope this timeless classic has sparked your imagination and enriched your literary journey. Now that you've turned the final page, we want to share a vision for the future of reading—one where every classic you've ever wanted to explore is at your fingertips, in a format that best suits your life.

We'd like to invite you to gain immediate, unlimited digital & audiobook access to hundreds of the most treasured literary classics ever written—along with the option to secure deluxe paperback, hardcover & box set editions at printing cost. Together, we can spark a new global literary renaissance alongside our small, independent publishing house called "The Library of Alexandria."

Thousands of years ago, the Library of Alexandria stood as a beacon of knowledge—until it was lost to history. We aim to reignite that spirit of preservation and discovery right now, in the modern age—only this time, it's accessible to all, in every language and every format.

Picture a world where every timeless classic, novel, poem, or philosophical treatise is not only available to read but also updated for today's readers—modernized, translated into any language or dialect, and ready to enjoy in any format you choose, whether that is in an eBook, audiobook, paperback, or deluxe hardcover & box set version a printing cost.

By joining our movement to rebuild the modern Library of Alexandria, you become part of an unprecedented mission to offer:

- **Unlimited Audiobook & eBook Access to the Greatest Classics of All Time**

    Instantly explore thousands of legendary works, from Plato and Shakespeare to Jane Austen and Leo Tolstoy. All are instantly ready to read or listen to, giving you a complete literary universe at your fingertips.

- **Paperback & Deluxe Editions at Printing Costs:**

    Purchase any title in a paperback, deluxe hardbound, or deluxe boxset edition at printing costs, shipped right to your doorstep. Curate your personal library of Alexandria with editions worthy of display—crafted to last, designed to captivate, and delivered straight to your door.

- **Modern translations for Contemporary Readers in all languages and dialects**

    Discover a vast selection of classics reimagined in clear, current language—no more struggling with outdated phrases or obscure references. Next to the original versions, we aim to offer translations in as many languages and dialects as possible.

    As we continue our translation efforts and add new languages, readers everywhere can connect with these works as if they were written today. By bridging linguistic divides, you're contributing to ensuring that these timeless stories become more meaningful, accessible, and inspiring for people across the globe.

- **Your Personal Library of Alexandria:**

    Over the months and years, you'll curate a unique physical archive of classics—each volume a testament to your taste, curiosity, and love of knowledge. It's not just about owning books—it's about curating a cultural legacy you'll cherish and pass down for generations to come.

- **Join a Global Literary Renaissance:**

    Your support fuels an ongoing mission: allowing us to reinvest in offering deluxe print editions (including special boxsets) at their true cost, broaden the range of available formats and translations, and extend the reach of these works to new audiences worldwide. By joining today, you're not just preserving a legacy of masterpieces; you set in motion a powerful wave of literary accessibility.

We are more than a publisher—we're a movement, and we can't do it alone. Your support lets us scale our mission, preserving and reimagining history's greatest works for tomorrow's readers.

Become a Torchbearer of knowledge.

Thank you for picking up this book and allowing us into your literary journey. As you turn the pages, know that you're part of something larger: a global effort to keep these stories alive, share their wisdom across borders and generations, and spark a true cultural revival for the modern era.

If this resonates with you—please consider taking the next step by visiting:

www.libraryofalexandria.com

With gratitude and a shared love of knowledge,

The Modern Library of Alexandria Team

Visit:

www.libraryofalexandria.com

Or scan the code below:

www.ingramcontent.com/pod-product-compliance
Lightning Source LLC
LaVergne TN
LVHW030632080426
835512LV00021B/3468